A Pen to A Pad

෴ ❖ ෴

Don't Die Without A Loving Heart

Alina Hopgood

Table of Contents

Abide In Love 1	Captured 40
Officially Confused 2	You Took the Blame 42
Confused 4	Consistent in My Pursuit 44
Just a Dream 6	It's All Beautiful 47
Finally 8	When I Asked 48
Our God is Great 10	This Path I'm On 50
His Quest 12	I am Overwhelmed 53
The LORD Made 13	Don't Tell Me 54
In Your Will 14	You Have My Heart 56
Prepare Yourself 17	You Are 58
What About Forever 18	See What Could Be 59
We Did This Together 20	From the Beginning 60
How It Is 22	Glory Awaits Us 62
Same Place 24	Living Water 64
I Can Not Read Your Mind 26	Move Forward Or Die 66
How Could You – And I Not 28	You Will Become 68
Goin' Off 30	Beginning At the End 70
Without Thinking 32	Natural Disaster 72
On a Cloud 34	Irresistible 74
To the Top 36	How Deep 76
The Soul Knows 38	

My Dedication

This book is dedicated to those who love hard, no matter the cost. Those who take advantage of the opportunities granted to them to make someone else feel special despite that individual's nature or past. Those who truly believe that love will always win in the end. Never stop writing!

~ Alina

Abide In Love

Our love is strong
Our love is pure
It's unconditionally constant
Constant as day returns to night
Our love holds us together with all its might
How can love change a spirit?
Make a spirit unload its selfishness?
This is the miracle of it
This is the purpose of it
Love never fails
You can count on it
So, love all you can
Get all the love upon you given
He who abides in love,
Abides in God
And God in him.

Officially Confused

I'd like to know what happened
I thought we were lifelong friends
We spent quality time together
And now I'm lost, because it somehow ends.
The reason why, I'm unsure of
The way it went down is unheard of
I'm in shock, my mind is cluttered
All of this time, I thought we were in love.
The reassurance I had given
The confidence in us was not hidden
Kept me going, my heart beating
Hope we'd last forever, together livin'
You've killed that dream
Inside my soul screams
This was not what I expected
How could you just walk out on me?
My phone works well
I still check my email
Even the spam!
So just who did you tell?
The closure I needed was not an option
You change your mind like it's a routine; often.
I'm left sitting here all alone
When I gave my heart to you – there was no sign that read
CAUTION!
What in the world did I say?
Was I acting a weird way?

Did you disagree with my lifestyle?
I honestly felt we were on the same page
Did I skip a word?
Was a verb unheard?
Lord, reveal it; answer me
Did I miss a turn?
I am not at anyone's disposal
I love me more than anyone's proposal
I love me more
So, if it's over; let it be done
Let it be official
Because I'm officially confused.

Confused

So, remind me again
I need to understand
You say that you want an independent female
Well, here I am

I can take care of my own
God is first in my home
I am blessed to be intellectual
I am grown

Why are you running away?
I am the result of what you pray
Are you scared?
I'll help you to not be so afraid

Love is all I desire inside
Someone I can trust in and confide
Does that matter to you
Or are you looking with a naked eye?

Where is your depth of character?
Why be so shallow?
Everything you need is right before you
But you'd rather eat junk food

I can't say that I'm confused
But I think you are
And I can't say I feel any pain
But I know you are
To be given what you ask for
Then get rid of what you should adore
I feel sorry for you, because of your stupidity
Usually if a treasure is lost
That loser weeps

Just a Dream

Last night I had a dream
Waking up unsure of what it could mean
The characters involved were no mystery
Everything was so clear and vivid to me
Emotions were shown from my end
And they received what I had sent
So, now confusion has erupted
And since I told him, now I'm busted
But was it only just a dream
Or is much more to be redeemed?
I confessed those 3 tiny words
And only my sub-conscience heard
But my heart beat to a fast-paced rhythm
And my head ached when I awoke to realism

It was only a dream

It was only a dream

What a relief. I can go back to sleep

And dream a little dream of me

But I feel something has been unleashed

He doesn't know it was just a dream

That felt so real to me

Inside my fantasy, I'm weightless

Weightless to the pressure of never sharing my feelings

So I go on and let him know

Let the words flow freely

I'm not let down by his rejection

I've made up my own reflection of him

So I can say what I want

I can be who I want

It was only just a dream.

Finally

Excitement is overwhelming me

My pulse is racing faster than a speeding bullet

Finally is the only word to describe

All the dreams and wishes I hold inside

Coming true finally

Being with you finally

Wild birds roam free

Take risks and trail their curiosity

Knowing home is just a flight away

No matter how dark the night or bright the day

Their identity never changed

Even if wild birds all look the same

So many possibilities of where it can go

Been a lot of places, but still there's no place like home

I've got both feet on the ground

I can only move forward now

And hum a tune made up internally

It's time to follow my dreams finally

My heart is sound and is expecting

It knows what it wants and is getting

My mind has invited in optimistic thoughts

No vacancy for procrastination or sin

Finally I can begin

I see the true ways of the world

I am aware of the traps beset upon me

I am maneuvering unafraid

No doubts, no hesitation, strategies are made

Moving forward finally

Never going back ever

I'm happy finally

Our God is Great

As I sit out here and gaze
The wind gently caressing my face
God is truly great
Our God is great
I stretch my arms out far and wide
Deeply inhaling; looking towards the sky
I am truly alive
Thank God I'm alive
If you've never gone through a drought
How could you know what the feeling of a flood is all about?
Being content with the little blessings
Makes you humble for the bigger delicacies
God is truly great
Our God is great
As I reflect on what I don't deserve
All the tribulations and how He preserved
Reserved me to fulfill my purpose
When I could have seen myself as worthless
But God is truly great
Our God is great

I can write it no other way
I am grateful You never turned away
The more of You I seek after
To see what You see
To know what You know
To help You fill each day with hope and laughter
You've loved me forever
No matter. Whatever.
God, in You, I increase my faith
I decrease, move myself out of Your way
God is truly great
Our God is great

His Quest

I hear a knock at the door

I dare not ignore

For behind this wall could be my fate

I can not wait

Love has come on a long journey my way

I hope and pray

"Who is it?" I so anxiously imply

I can't figure out why

Already turning the knob to open, I proceed

My heart's racing at top speed

I'm taken by surprise

I can not believe my eyes

I'm swept up off my feet

For his lips and mine meet

He's mine to cherish and keep

I care to weep

Tears fall from my eyes like rain

He's erased my pain

I welcome him in to rest

I am the destination to his quest

The road was long and windy

Glad he made it finally

A lot of knocks went unanswered

They could not enter

Just as the rhythm my heart beats

So is the rhythm my ears seek

When you knocked simultaneously

I swear my heart skipped a beat

The LORD Made

This is the day that the LORD made
That the LORD made
The LORD made
So what makes you say,
"This is the worst day"?
When so often
We go about our day never giving Him the praise
Never noticing the ways
The LORD made
This is not the hour to mourn
But rather a time to die and be reborn
To receive the gift that was not cheap
The LORD paid to set you free
The worst day for you is when you do not take heed
His word is clear to you
Everyday you simply breathe
This is the day that the LORD made
That the LORD made
The LORD made
Quit murmuring and complaining
Where is that taking you in a hurry?
Stop, thank Him, and don't worry

In Your Will

When I am in Your will
I have joy everlasting
I have peace outlasting
I worry not about the next day
I see You moving in every way
Pulling down strong holds
Making me pure gold

When I am in Your Will
My purpose is revealed
The debt I owe for sin is repealed
I look toward the light
Where there is light, there is life
Light makes known all that is hidden
Living in darkness is forbidden

When I am in Your will
I am covered
The mystery of You is uncovered
I take rest in Your presence
I give You reverence
I close my eyes to worship
I lift my hands for You to show up

When I am in Your Will
Everything is right and perfect
I am not entranced by the worlds' direct

My faith in man is nonexistent
My only source is Omniscient
Whatever You say is true
You know exactly what to do

When I am in Your Will
Who can stand against me?
Whose side already has the victory?
Angels will take charge
I am neither afraid of the adversary nor alarmed
You take control in all my situations
You show yourself strong and mighty in my defense

When I am in Your Will
I dare not step out on my own
Failure is forthcoming by me alone
I follow the path You have strategically set
For with my own direction, I've experienced regret
You knew that was needed for my recruitment
I will never move again without Your consent

When I am in your Will
Love is acted out
It suffers long and never leaves a doubt
It is who You are, what You are
And it is where You are
That is where I abide
In You, is where I hide

I count it all joy to walk in Your Will
I will praise You even still
When I can't see tomorrow
When I can't see; I'll just follow
Whatever You say is what I will do
Yes LORD, my will, I lay waste to.

"As for God, his way is perfect; the word of the LORD is flawless. He is a shield for all who take refuge in him." 2 Samuel 22.31

Prepare Yourself

Are we prepared for the future?

Being conscious of what it will bring.

Considering the consequences of not caring?

Do you realize the impact you make

Even when you do absolutely nothing?

Freedom comes with knowledge

Good crops grow from good ground

Have you planted for the harvest?

Imitate the good habits of prosperous people.

Joke not about being wise.

Keep your mouth off of "do-gooders"

Leave the past failures there

Move forward on a new path

Never sin.

Open your heart up again.

Prepare yourself for the final return

Question not about whether it will be so

Rebuke, reprove, and oppose unholy things

Save yourself.

Trembling and gnashing of teeth is what you'll do in hell.

Uphold, undergird yourself with truth

Visualize your eternity

What are you prepared for?

X-out sin, expect redemption and accept forgiveness

You are chosen by God to do great things

Zero in, concentrate on Him, and He will take care of it all.

What About Forever

Perhaps I was mistaken

Or was looking through a broken glass

The reflection I saw coming off of that mirror

Must have been appearances of us from the past

I try not to think about yesterday

But it keeps coming back

Are you experiencing the same difficulty?

Are you too scared to act?

You focus on other pursuits now

Try to distract yourself from the truth

I can see that it's not successful

But you are the only one with the power over you

My mind is clear

I can move on if I wanted to

Time is a constant upward movement

Yet I'm still sitting here waiting on you

Perhaps I'm in denial

My closure session has not begun

All of my questions have not been discussed

How can you just move on?

Does that mean what you said is invalid?

Have all the passwords changed?

What about forever?

Did you mean it's forever as long as you stayed the same?

I don't know how to love you anymore

You've switched channels and I've lost the remote

Or did you take that as well?

Maybe that's why our hearts are at war

I'm in foreign territory

Languages and customs all disagree

I didn't think this could ever happen

I couldn't imagine how this would even come to be

I give you back your key

It's time to wake up, face reality

The show must go on

We Did This Together

We were able to laugh.
Able to cry
Able to dance
Able to celebrate our lives
We did all this together
Never ruffled any feathers
We were able to pray
Able to enjoy well-prepared food
Able to go our separate ways
Able to see through all the bad to the good
We did all this as a family
Loving one another truly and deeply
Looking into the eyes of another
You can see we are so much alike
We add depth to one another's personality
I walk this way because of this reason
I talk this way because of that reason
We begin to clarify and become defined

We are able to be ourselves
Able to have fun
Able to be sophisticated
Able to love beyond all wrongs
We did all this together
Never forgetting we are a family
When the curtain falls
When the lights go dim
When we are shut off from the rest of the world
Able to be transparent
Our bonds will not be broken
Our chains will not snap
We will always have each other
And that is that

How It Is

He loves me not
Will always be unheard words
For the way that he acknowledges me
He loves me more
I am astounded by his interest
His investment to learn me
He looks at me like no one else could
And accepts me simply
I am the treasure in his chest
I am a significant symbol in his crest
He defines my beauty as his best
And strives to treat me like nothing less
He loves me
In every way
I never have to change
Improvement wouldn't cause damage or strain
But either way, his adoration is still the same
I am his for a lifetime
Wish there could be more time
To have his presence in my life
When you are young and naïve
You wish for everything to be the way of society
When you mature, you begin to see
None of that can estimate or define
The love that two share or their identity
This is not an experiment
This is real
Nor is it a matter of what you can get out of it
This is truly how I feel

Our casual friendship was no mistake
We were one from the start; we could relate
That's something rare to find
Some may seem to scrutinize
But I know you and you know I
So what's the basis for even asking why?
I'm done plucking this flower
I don't care what the final petal may reveal
I know that I love you
This was not a complicated gospel to instill
I have and always will continue to be your friend
Love conquers all
I'm a witness together with you
We have already defeated the opposition
We will win.

Same Place

I never thought this day would come

Of course, the Man upstairs did.

You and I are in the same place.

On one accord

You know me yet we've never met

I'm fantasizing about my future once again

My dreams have been refreshed

My love has been renewed

My happiness has been restored

Now that you and I are in the same place

What is going to happen now?

Why must that establishment be a priority?

I am just enjoying the moments I have

To see you smile.

To see you laugh.

To see you walk.

To see you be you.

The one I like the most.

Too many words will just bring confusion

Too many thoughts will just bring frustration

Let's just be in the same place

I see you

And you see me

Hurts and obstacles have brought us here

We are certainly being careful,

Which is what I love the most

I never thought this day would come

I give God all the praise

For you and I are in the same place

It's pure opportunity

Do you see what I see?

I may be crazy

But when you're in love there's only one way you can be

You get nervous around them

You can't help but smile

You think about them constantly

No one - sane - does this stuff

It's blissful insanity

When you and I are in the same place

I never want to leave.

I Can Not Read Your Mind

I can not read your mind

Although I try

I am unsuccessful somehow

Tell me all that I am to know

Don't leave me alone

To dig through this closet that is piled high

With thoughts and feelings never hired

They are all expired.

Can I get rid of them for you?

All of the expectations;

All of the rejections

Boxes and bags of misplaced love;

Misplaced attention

All of the questions

I can not read your mind

You must tell me

The only release that you have

Hear yourself say these things

Hear yourself cry out

Hear yourself bring healing

Open all the doors in your house

Let fresh air in

Let it all hang out

You have my shoulder

You have my ear

You have me willing

To just be here

I know what it takes to help you renew

God has given me a gift

I will share all that I have with you

One step must be taken on your part

I can not read your mind

Take the step to open up to me

Let me know your heart

Invite me to sit in your home

Give me the grand tour

I love you beyond you

Nothing surprises me ever

So, let the aggression of my love for you surprise you

How Could You – And I Not?

How could You make me – and I not recognize You?

How could You give me existence – and I not even say thank You?

I did not get here on my own

Nor is my purpose grounded in myself

I am Yours

I may have been stolen for a time

But I'm free

And I run back into Your arms

Into Your protection

Into Your consideration

I have been lost for a time

I chose not to see You

I was in darkness and didn't even know it

I owe You my life

You didn't allow me to die in my filth

You came to my rescue

What mercy You've given

I am in deep gratitude

I am in awe of You

You are omniscient

You knew me before I knew me

I am still learning me

But I rely on You now

To tell me who I am

Tell me why You thought of me

And how I fit in the grand scheme of things

You don't make mistakes
And I'm so glad You've already counted me in
I get into situations
Only You can pull me out of
Big God
Little me
How could You save me – and I not worship You?
How could You be so faithful – and I neglect You without even caring?
How could You just forgive me?
I'm so inconsiderate of Your feelings
I don't thank You when You wake me from a deep sleep
I don't thank You when the food is there
I don't go to You with my problems
But I run quick to tell a friend –
What can they do about it?
I don't give You what I owe; yet You give me what I shouldn't get
I'm not grateful with the little I have
And my greed leads me to fail
My pride prevents me from apologizing
How could You love me like You do – and I not accept it?
I am a dumb sheep
You are the good Shepherd
I am relieved to know that my life
Is being guided and taken care of by You, God.

Goin' Off

Your actions are speaking louder

Your words are like piercing swords to my ears

You keep me expecting more

And I'm foolish enough to do it anyway

Why am I here?

What is my purpose?

Am I doing something wrong?

Something wrong always occurs

"Can't get right!"

Yes, I can!

I can choose what I will do

I can change my mood

I don't have to let it effect me

But every time, somehow, I do

I let your actions get to me

And my ears slowly begin to bleed

Excruciating pain

Make it stop!

You tell me one thing and yet you do another

Is that an easy task?

You make it look less complex

Than an open heart surgery

But somehow the severity of it is equal

I make my point

You make yours

No conclusion to the matter

I shed my tears

You punch the wall

And still no solution

I'm done with expectations

I'm through thinking that you'll be different

I keep getting my hopes up

So stop lying to me

Prove it to me

Words mean nothing to me

Actions are the true reflection of your words

Mirror, mirror on the wall

What are your words going to look like today?

Without Thinking

Come unto me

Listen to me speak

Incline and you will hear

My soft, sweet voice enter your ear

I think of quiet nights

Stars ever so bright

Enjoying my life with you

Taking it easy and being true

You have been honest with me

I can ask for no other way to be

Now I must reciprocate this manner

You must know how much to me you matter

You matter more than sun to begin each morning

You matter more than money to function in society

You matter more than music to express our joy and mourning

You matter more than tears to convey feelings too strong to speak

I tell you everything I think

Everything I dream

No matter how distasteful or horrific it may seem

I am compelled to tell thee

When you begin to wonder about it and count the what ifs

That's when you've allowed for doubt

I was not thinking when I told you,

I loved you

I was not analyzing my approach or tone

I simply became a great friend to you

I was loyal

I was true

It was easy gaining my feelings

The more time spent with you

The closer we grew
I never thought you'd matter
I never thought
So now I'm foolishly thinking of reasons
The many reason to not let this be
I am thinking which in itself is foolish
Your mind never knows what your heart's desire is
This is why I speak from my heart
Just like it was from the start
From the start, we've come this far
Not looking at how things will be
No expectations.
Just us
Just honesty
Without thinking

On a Cloud

I'm floating on a cloud
I'm so high, I'm looking down
Below I see
Many odd things
Like sorrowful people
No smiling
Stressed about money
Division among families
There's darkness everywhere
Something major would have to happen for people to even care
Why God must it come to this point?
My God, where is the light?
Why are so many people distracted or deceived?
They don't even realize how they're living
I float on a cloud
And pray with all hope and no doubt
Make the disturbance cease
Let the light in their hearts increase
Let that same light shine so bright
Eyes of the wicked become opened
Wipe away the tears of the depressed
Relieve the pressures of provision in this economy from the distressed.

Do it now, LORD!
I believe all the promises You made in Your word
I'm stepping down out of this cloud
I will be glad about this change and proud
Earth is preparation for our true happiness
Heaven can only give that
We only make it to Heaven from down here
Based on how we live
God can renew our strength
If you were on a cloud gazing down at your life,
What would you see?

To the Top

When you get to the top
Don't forget to look down
Don't allow yourself to get so high
That you still can't reach the ground
Remain humble
Always share
And if someone needs help
Show them that you care

When you get to the top
Don't forget to look down
Give what you have to the poor
Don't be a selfish clown
Let your height
Give you more access
To do good things
In a time when bad is causing mess

When you get to the top
Don't forget to look down
To notice the mortals who look up to you
Who knew you before you grew
Thank the disciplinarians
For their achievements
Reprimanding you
Preparing you to face this challenge
For believing in your future
Keeping you balanced

When you get to the top
I hope you won't stop climbing
Don't forget to look down
You're moving in perfect timing.

The Soul Knows

She glanced in his direction
To behold a handsome creation
Her eyes were attached to this rarity
And dreams formed within her soul
His eyes were drawing her intrigue
The sincerity of it all made her weep

If his beauty could make her weep
She thought she ought to move in his direction
To appeal to her curiosity; build her intrigue
He is solely God's creation
Fashioned and formed externally to capture his soul
She absolutely belongs with this rarity

Can't even fathom an ordinary rarity
That alone could cause an involuntary weep
He's made for her complete; the mate to her soul
Her appeal was denied; he ambled her direction
To boast about the joy of God's creation
As he held her hand and looked in intrigue

They were on a quest compelled by unlimited intrigue
To satisfy the value of their exclusive rarity
Love was pledged and began a new creation
This overwhelming joy caused them both to weep
Her glance, his approach, has led in this direction
The path that is only known by the soul

Now he and she are one soul
With undying intrigue
She follows his lead as he follows God's direction
Never escaping from the memory of their rarity
Her tears must form the words as she can only weep
He gives away the bride of their creation

She beholds this wonderful, beautiful creation
Proud of the humble, maturity of the soul
He sees her heart through her weep
She longs to forever bask in his intrigue
His choice is to reverence her rarity
Never looking to destruct the path's passionate direction

A rarity this fascinating is a true creation
Brought about by intrigue that causes one to weep
Appreciating every direction never misled by the soul

"Captured"

You have captured my attention
My sacrifice is simply a privilege
One that I don't deserve
For I've done some shameful things
Which I can only blame myself
But I leave that in the past to rest
And I bring to life true feelings and intentions for you alone

You have captured my attention
The more I'm in your presence
The larger my attraction grows
And when I'm away for no matter how long
The harder it gets being apart
And it hits me just how much I care
I am glad

You have captured my attention
Increased my interest
Broadened my horizon
Have been my hope and inspiration to follow my dreams
Given me the opportunity to choose to give you my heart
Which I desire to do

You have captured my attention
Blocked out all distractions
I feel the need to be near you
I see no one else, but you
I soak up each tear that falls from your eyes
They are absorbed by the roots of my intrigue
Until it is mature

You have captured my attention
There is no turning back to nothing
When completeness is right in front of me
You fascinate me
You challenge me
I listen to your soul calling for mine
And I answer back with this line

"You have captured my attention!"

You Took the Blame

For a time and a purpose, we were created
With all reason and without excuse, we praise
Our hands were formed to be our weapons
Our mouths sing and shout with joy
We can do nothing or even breathe without Him
For my salvation, You took the blame

For my disobedience, You took the blame
You laid down your life before we were created
You knew there'd come a time we'd need Him
Our time of sacrifice is now and our sacrifice is praise
Praise with all we have in the spirit of joy
My praise and worship are my weapons

I'll let no deceptive demon get hold of my weapons
When I sin, I'll repent and take the blame
I'll accept my forgiveness in truth with joy
My strength comes from the one in Whose image I'm created
I was created to love; indebted to give praise
For no glory of my own – it all belongs to Him

I will keep my mind stayed on Him
In His Word; my sword, my weapons
Walls fall down and crumble when I praise
The strongholds are broken and no more is the blame
This is the true life God intended and created
So that we would have fullness of joy

Unspeakable joy
Strength and peace in Him
Pre-destined and created
Equipped with spiritual weapons
No longer accepting or inheriting the blame
With all I am, I give the Lord praise

For all I have, I give Him praise
My strength relies upon His joy
It's my entire fault, yet innocent, You took the blame
I long to be closer to Him
I'll fight to keep Him; I'll utilize my weapons
Everything is good that God created

I am created to never stop my praise
For these weapons are mighty through Him
I have joy continually. You took the blame.

"God made him who had no sin to be sin for us, so that in him we might become the righteousness of God." 2 Corinthians 5.21 NIV

"For the weapons of our warfare are not carnal, but mighty through God to the pulling down of strong holds;" 2 Corinthians 2.4 KJV

Consistent in My Pursuit

I don't change with the wind's direction
I am consistent in my pursuit of perfection

Can you see in my eyes, the innocence?
I'm not fooled by your charming sentences

Heard it all before. Even more,
I've seen it first hand! Nevermore walking through that door.

To the top of this ladder of chance, I must climb.
I must climb to the top of this ladder; it's my time.

I'm prepared for this journey
Like a hiker with gear in a hurry

I'm trying to go far in a short amount of time
Everyone says, "Slow down girl! This ain't no mother goose rhyme!"

I've got somewhere to be
I won't be late, neither will he.

I sit in front of this empty plate.
The Master chef works His best to create.

I covet no menu to order from
He's got me taken care of and then some

I stand in the midst of an ever-changing wind
It's trying to cajole me. After all, isn't that the purpose of a trend?

A trend shifts and changes with the climate
It will be all you see currently whether you do or don't like it.

In my own strength; I'm weak.
In my own confidence is conceit.

In my own direction; I'm lost.
With my own eyes, I'm seeing crisscrossed.

Trusting in human wisdom; utter sin
Me getting the glory; Satan's win

I will not be tossed and driven.
I realize the mercy I've been given.

I will move when He says move.
When He says move, that's what I'll do.

One will uniquely complete me
A precisely cut and chiseled masterpiece

Master, please send him vastly
Quicker than a girl rolling her eyes and being chastised for being sassy.

This is all that I would ask
Everything for You is a possible task

I stand on Your word and not in Your way
I'll allow You to speak and hear what You say

I am consistent in my pursuit of perfection
I evaluate my intentions; the important section

On the way to my destination,
Rains will pour and winds will bring devastation

I will not be moved from where I stand
Following directions like an instrument in a band

I'll cry my tears of sorrow
I'll look forward to every tomorrow

This will be the greatest journey ever travelled.
Ever travelled, this will be the greatest journey as it's unraveled.

It's All Beautiful

It's all beautiful in My eyes
Because I see well into the future
I see where you're coming from
I see all the good that's bound to come

It's all beautiful in My eyes
What seems tragic at the time
I will use your pain to get you prepared
For the even greater purpose that I see

It's all beautiful in My eyes
What seems to you to be only a mystery
You can not uncover what is in storage for you
I can only give it at the appointed time

Everything has an appointed time
A time to be born and a time to die
A time to mourn and to celebrate
A time to plant and to enjoy the fruit of that plant
It's all beautiful in My eyes

At the designated time
In My good judgment
I will remove the blindfold from your eyes
You will have clear vision
You will be able to appreciate all of the beauty
But for now, My dear one, just trust Me
It all looks beautiful from here to Me

~God

When I Asked

I heard someone say, "Be careful what you pray for,
Because you just might get it."

Although, I never believed it was true,
The more I prayed to God, the more I received it.

I asked the LORD for wisdom
He began to open my eyes and ears to knowledge
He showed me the areas where I was ignorant and foolish.

It appeared to me that I was beginning a new journey.
Learning things that I had always heard, but never quite understood.

So I kept on asking God for more, because I knew He would listen!

I asked God for deliverance from past hurts and depression caused by my failures.

Words were spoken into my life by various people
Words of Hope
Forgiveness
Restoration
People who were not privy to my struggles were encouraging me in God.

I could instantly see my transformation!

He was breaking the chains
Chains that were causing my feet to lay dormant;
Stopping my arms from operating
Until then, I could not do the will of my Father
Until then, I could not live for I was a slave to sin.

So I asked the LORD what to do with my money

He gave me a simple formula
Now, I lack nothing. I am blessed.
I give to Him first and He takes care of the rest.

He doesn't require much, just a heart of worship.
He desires such that we commune with Him.

By having faith that my prayers are being answered,
I speak the things I want in my life
Not the things that bring disaster

Our faith makes us right with Jesus
And the prayer of a righteous man avails much!

What you say will come your way!

LORD, I pray that this reader is blessed.
Let their prayers be heard and let the answers be revealed in due time.
Let them be careful in what they petition.
All praise, glory, and honor belong to You.

"And without faith it is impossible to please God,
because anyone who comes to him must believe that he exists
and that he rewards those who earnestly seek him."
Hebrews 11.6 NIV

This Path I'm On

I'm furious with frustration
I can't concentrate, because of the conditions
I'm under,
Under pressure
I'm visibly voluntarily looking okay with everything
I know how to look less longing to lock myself away
From the pressure
From the stress
Seeing you standing there sincerely seeking to see me naked
Totally truthful with your temptations to tear off my clothes
I'm in a whirlwind of lustful words
One takes me up and the next brings me down
It twists and twirls me upside down
Then unintentionally turns me off
Now I sit on the floor of my emotions
Feeling taken advantage of by your advances
Driving down a dead end road to the dark side
My worth will not be washed away with guilt
Work for what you want
How else will you wantonly appreciate it?
My choice to chase after a charming Chico
Changes your chance of climbing to my level, Rico
Suave, right?
Well, you can call me Frank Sinatra
'Cause frankly I sin not, trust.
One thing you must never misinterpret
I'll lay my love upon you unconditionally
But my body abides by ancient breeding rules

The basics are One woman for One man

One vow, one ring, one unit, one blessing

There's no other equation equal that God created

So, one man for one man

Or one woman for one woman

Or one man for two women equals nothing.

That's a whole lot of nothing.

Who lives to achieve the success of dying and getting nothing?

Count the costs.

Could you come up with the cash

Or would you need credit?

I'm in misdeed debt desiring to be delivered

And you desire to drive me right to the damnable den

With your disobedient directions for me to get undressed

Carefully you could care less about me

Stuck out on the sea of your selfishness

Where my frustration lies

I'm seasick seeing how sick you are

I vomit your venomous verbs, not built to ingest vanity

I run after righteousness

Relying on repentance to render me relief

Bring me safely to shore

I took a chance hoping for the best of someone

But he only hoped for the worst from me

This probably happens to God everyday

Used for what He can do well.

Never willingly worshipped whenever

Instead avariciously asked at all hours

I feel your pain, LORD.

People perish for a lack of knowledge

I'm glad Your grace goes a good way off
Beyond the good way off, we've gone.
I'm on the path to please Yahweh
Please pause in your passion to appease your flesh
While grabbing my hand to guide me to your dead end, fool.
I'm not easily enticed by your enthusiastic expressions
Against all evil a standard is lifted on my behalf.
So, I think I am all right with staying on this path
This path will lead me to His good graces.
You're welcome to join me.

Hosea 4.6a *"My people are destroyed for a lack of knowledge…"*

Genesis 2.24 *"Therefore a man shall leave his father and mother and be joined to his wife, and they shall become one flesh."*

2 Timothy 3:1-3 *"1) But mark this: There will be terrible times in the last days. 2) People will be lovers of themselves, lovers of money, boastful, proud, abusive, disobedient to their parents, ungrateful, unholy, 3) without love, unforgiving, slanderous, without self-control, brutal, not lovers of the good,"*

Proverbs 8.20 *"I walk in righteousness, in paths of justice."*

I am Overwhelmed

I am overwhelmed
My heart is ready for love
Right when I gave up on the feeling
You came along and began to sing
Your sweet voice rang in my ears
More and more how I want you near
I realize that it wasn't physical
You were humming to my spiritual
Spirit to spirit, I sense you
It's so sincere
I begin to dance to your song
I sway and I move
The more I move, the closer I get to you
You noticed me in the crowd
You picked me out the crowd
Now we dance together
We hold hands and sway together
I am overwhelmed
My heart is yours to love
I trust that you will not…
You will not all of the will not's
And I will do all the will do's
Especially the I do's
I will calmly and patiently be yours
You just keep singing to me
You've gone beyond my expecting
I love being with you
I love you

Don't Tell Me

Don't tell me you love me

But are not willing to fight to keep me

Or die to redeem me

When my heart is losing vitality,

Why aren't you there to revive me?

When times are hard to find your touch

Why do you disconnect from me more?

Why when I bring up the honest truth

Why do you run away in avoidance?

Are you scared to face the truth?

We can't live in La-La Land forever.

My heart is in need of reassurance

My soul needs to feel yours.

Don't let this love drown in a sea of fear

Don't let fear hinder us from being mature

I need for us to mature.

I need for our love to remain strong.

If we never go through anything together,

How will we ever grow together?

If you search for an escape route now

Where will you be when I'm under attack?

When I question my destiny with you?

When I have doubts about being in love?

Will you be there to assure?

Will your inner level of care measure up to your external actions?

Don't tell me you love me,

If you don't know what that means.

Love bears all things…

It encounters all things and endures all things.

Our encounter has come to a test

Will you endure with me?
Will you suffer through to become one?
When you were alone, on a soul search
Trying to find out who you are and why you're here
You had challenges, obstacles, heart breaks
You became stronger as a person.
Your character was produced.
Apply the same principle here.
We go through things together,
To become stronger as one, a team, a companionship.
If you will not die for me, be selfless for me
You can not love me.
I will cross the ocean for you
I will visit any country you desire
I will give my life for you,
if that's what is required to gain your love and trust.
I hope that I never have to,
Because I will never get to experience it.
So, love me now. Trust me now. Bear with me.
This is totally a spiritual battle
The devil doesn't want to see love succeed; better yet, even exist.
I will fight for Love; I will do all I can.
When I get tired, I need you to step in.
Step up and remind me why we're fighting so hard

You Have My Heart

You have my heart
You ignite my life's flame
In the center of my joy, You sit
In the river of my peace, You swim
In the cool breeze of a hot day
You are the wind that blows me away
You knock me over with Your love
You captivate me with Your love
Your thoughts transcend even the wisest person's
Making them look elementary
You need no one else's help or expertise
You alone can part the seas
The same God Who created the sun
and fashioned its design and purpose
Is the very same God Who saw it in
His plan to create little me
You are my Creator, the King, royalty
I'm honored to be crafted by You
To be considered by You each day
To be known by You

You have my heart
You ignite my life's flame
I am a city on a hill for You
Lit by the flame of Your glory
Kept lit by the assistance of Your grace
Never destroyed by the evil one
Rather employed to destroy the evil one
You employed me
You gave me full benefits
And best of all, when I retire
You have a mansion built just for me
I don't know of any other boss
Who can heal you
Who will be patient for however long it takes for you to get it
Who knows the number of hairs on your head
Who gave you a name that's unique to you
In the novel of my faith,
You write every sentence.

You Are

Your eyes show me your soul
Your lips tell me your goal
Your feet lead me to our destination
Your hands secure me like my protection
Your initiative is amazingly intriguing
It keeps me breathlessly wondering
You have no uncertainty about me
As if God spoke to you directly about me
He described what I would look like, feel like, smell like
How I would complete you
How I'd be blessed beyond imagination when I'd finally meet you.
I've guarded my heart with high-level security limits
Access is granted to only one exact match that exists
The man of my dreams - you are
The exact identity - you are
The one with full access to my heart - you are
The easiest man to love - you are
I've always believed in there being one man for me
One true love, one destiny
Now we've reached the place where our feet can land.
As we place our hearts in each other's hands
And watch our love grow to the highest and fullest it can.

See What Could Be

Open your eyes to see

That this could really be

Love can really bring about change

Love is the key

Love is the Name

Name me Joy

Name me Rain

But none is more powerful than that Name

Open your eyes to see

That this could really be

Really be the end of sorrow

Really see hope for tomorrow

This treacherous road of paralyzing potholes will come to a dead end

With one of two ways to follow

Open your eyes to see

That this could really be

Be nice to the winds of Change and Chance

Grab a kite and explore right where you stand

See the world and not just where you've seemed to land

You can be more

If you see more

The eyes of your optimism are shut

There is only one person who can forfeit this tournament of bad luck

If you'd just

Open your eyes to see

That this could really be

From the Beginning

Can we start from the beginning,
Before the apple was bitten and we were winning;
When love was all there was
And men and women could laugh together just because?
Can we go back to love's core?
No condemnation; No keeping score
What's mine is yours
And what His is ours; no divorce
We walked with God
We saw His face
All the glory and power
Now, we long to be back in that place
Where it all began
And we were all so grand
Now to sin, we enter in
No thinking twice of where it will end
Pleasures now
The future is blinded somehow
I don't want to imagine the risk
Others deny it and like the snake in the garden, at me, they hiss
Hiss…You don't drink?
Hiss…You don't smoke?
Yes, I don't stink.
And I won't croak.
Can we get away from all the hissing?
Can the world be removed from the list of the missing?

I am determined to get the crown
To lay it down
At the feet of the Savior
To cry Holy, Holy, Holy at His throne in His favor
I will do what's necessary
To be with Jesus even in the midst of the adversary
I am not deceived by his antagonistic ways
I know a God who can number the days.
We were sent here to bring back the strays
To keep Satan away
And I'm convinced the Son of God was sent
Not to prove only that God exists
But to bring the beginning back to the end
And now the love from the beginning
Is offered to us free from sinning
Therefore submit to God
Resist the devil and he will flee from you.
This is what the Lord says,
"If you return to me, I will restore you
So you can continue to serve me.
If you speak words that are worthy,
You will be my spokesman.
You are to influence them;
Do not let them influence you!"
We are greater than them,
Because the Greater One lives within
Let's get back to the beginning

Glory Awaits Us

Your wisdom and charm intrigue me
I am overtaken by your eyes as they speak to me
Your mouth never has to utter a word to solidify
However, whenever you do
I am more overtaken with joy and comfort
And my heart beats at a faster rhythm
My heart beats for you
Of you, I am in awe.
Each day, my love grows
From the soil of your commitment
And the water of your compassion
You count me in among the priority
You count me in
As if I am now on a team set out to dominate
Set out to win
I have played hard
I have loved hard
But to be on a team with equal fairness
I feel that the love I put forth is measured
Then given back with the same intensity
Same eagerness
Same anxiety
Same enthusiasm
Same carefulness
Same appreciation to God for his grace and favor
For there is nothing I could have ever done in my lifetime
To earn His grace for allowing me to be your woman
Nor did I ever ask to be given such a great man

I only asked for God to send me someone
Who would not dispose of my love
A man who would be able to understand the depth of who I am
A man with his own deep revelations for love and life
That we could expose our hearts and souls to each other
How was I supposed to know this would be the result?
Now I hold the key to your heart
As you hold the one to mine
We have a precious, fragile possession.
A lock that the other has the power to open
Releasing secrets and mysteries that have never been revealed
The truth of character, of feelings, of dreams, of hurts
We can unlock this hidden treasure
Add to it new crystal and precious stones of our own
I am overwhelmed with excitement
Ready for the adventure; the journey of love
Where in the end, glory awaits us

Living Water

Create in me, O LORD, a clean heart.
Let my actions display good motives.
Pour into my well a spring of living water.
Let it overflow, drowning my sorrow; killing all negativity.
I am desperate for water. I need to draw from the good Source.
I bring my vessel and lay it before Your throne.

I remove my jeweled crown and lay it at your gracious throne.
Please have a seat in the center of my heart.
I am hungry for the Bread of Life. For it, You are the only source.
Make my mind line up with Your thoughts and motives.
Replace mine with Your objectives - avoiding all negativity.
Remove the toxins and impurities with Your sanitizing water.

Rush over me, holy water.
Let the rivers flow straight from Your magnificent, royal throne.
Drown all sorrow, guilt, bitterness, jealousy, doubt, and negativity
So that I can smile from my heart
With joy and selfless, humane motives.
I am the resource, but You are the main source.

Maker of everything! The air we breathe – there is no other source.
I lift my hands and wait for You to release, over me, clear water
I commit my life unto You. Shield me from the enemy's motives.
Hide me and let me dwell in the secret place of Your throne.
Tell me Your secrets, LORD. Reveal the concerns of Your heart.
Teach me Your truth and love which block out negativity.

Your positive light infiltrates and drives out all negativity.
You are my reliable, immeasurable, uncontainable, amazing source.
Sit on the throne of my heart.
Holy Spirit, send thirst-quenching water.
Flow from my belly, O God, seated on the throne.
Your will is my will. I will accomplish Your motives.

With all my might, I will bring about Your motives.
Through me, You will break the energy of negativity.
Everlasting is Your throne!
Crushing are the waves of mighty water!
I tap into the source.
Create in me, O LORD, [my Maker] a relentless heart.

With a glad heart, let my actions stem from good motives.
Living water, rush in and drive out negativity.
God, You are the source. In the center of my life is Your throne.

"Jesus answered her, if you had only known and had recognized God's gift and Who this is that is saying to you, Give Me a drink, you would have asked Him [instead] and He would have given you living water."
John 4.10 AMP

Move Forward or Die

Moving forward is something we all have to do
Walk into the unknown
Claim new territory
Going back is not an option
Stalling will only get you killed
By the stampede of the forward-movers
Get your stuff and get going
Time is wasted the longer we stay here
The past was how it used to be
Good or bad it can not move
Locked away forever
What's left is present and future
Future promises, future hope,
Future blessings, future dreams
Don't get stuck in the dry cement of the past
Because you didn't keep moving forward
When the cement was still wet
It will take a whole crew to get you out now
And they could be spared having to hear the excuses
It's time to move forward, mature
Allow God to direct you
He has so many wonderful things in store for you

Put on your binoculars
Get a vision of what's ahead
It may seem too far to reach
But if you stay here, you'll never see
You'll never grow, you'll never know
You'll always be stuck in the old, in the dark
Light will move on without you
You will die in a cold, dark lifeless place
Have I convinced you yet?
Moving forward is necessary for survival
Evil lurks in dark cold places.
If evil is there that means God is not
To stay in His presence, we must keep moving
Renew our thinking
Light reveals truth and uncovers mysteries
You've got to stay in the knowledge
Don't deprive your self of fresh bread
Move forward
Depend on God
Be courageous
It won't be hard.

You Will Become

Do you even know what you could be?
The mirror that reflects your image
Is it the same one I see?

I see a marvelous work of art
Every particle strategically placed
The orchestrated pattern of your pulsating heart

You enjoy the music that you dance to
The food that you must eat to survive
You are a sight to see and a joy, too.

Do you even know what you could be?
Take one step outside yourself and look
You are intelligent and full of purity

I see a humble, sympathetic being
Unashamed to admit your mistakes
Willing to improve your manner of thinking

You are unique; you are on a mission
I am excited about what you'll become
You are purposed; you'll surpass the competition

Do you even know what you could be?
Can you understand your broad range of opportunity?
For someone like you, the possibilities are endless
You can make millions off of your brilliance

I see all of this inside of you
I decree and declare that every one of your dreams will come true.

Beginning at the End

I am seeking to find my purpose in life.
Life begins where sin ends.
My dreams, I need to see come true.
True happiness depends on it.
LORD, let Your will be done.
Done with the games and the compromise.
I am striving now.
Now is my time.
Catch me, LORD, if I should fall.
Fall upon me like the rain.
Give me Your peace,
Peace that goes beyond my understanding.
Take my hand, lead the way.
Way too many paths I can choose to take.
You know which one to travel.
Travel the narrower road with no distractions.
You will get there quicker and safer.
Safer in the righteousness of God.

That's where I long to abide.
Abide under the shadow of the Almighty.
Drowning in His grace and mercy
Mercy is shining like a light on me.
I will not let the worldly lusts influence.
Influence, I will, for the kingdom of God.
In the Kingdom, I am a beneficiary.
Beneficiary of His entire rich treasury
I want for nothing.
Nothing this world could offer will ever deter me.
I am seeking to find my purpose in God.
God begins when sin ends.

Natural Disaster

As the tears stream down like waterfalls

I try with all my strength to dam them

As I think about you

As I think about us

I was never afraid of falling in love with you

Nor was I afraid of letting you into my heart

What I fear now that we're apart

Is far worse than anything a person's heart should have to feel

A heart break.

Have you ever heard it?

A crack so loud it would blow your ear drums.

Have you felt that numbness?

Head-swelling numbness causes you to just lie down

I tried with all my might to avoid this

To stay in the fight.

To not let the devil win

To be committed until the end.

The end.

Is that a decision you make alone?

You sit and contemplate your phrases

You tell others' that have nothing to do with us

Get advice from friends and past lovers

And I'm given the final conclusion

And you have no regret

Was I that bad of a woman?

I'm not even worth that much respect?

I never cheated or lied or held back information

You deserved that as a man

You deserved the best in my eyes

A king in my eyes

You were supposed to be everything that God created you to be for me

Purposed for me in my eyes

Now I have these tears in my eyes

Replacing all of who you were in my eyes

And my levee is failing to hold them back

I'll let you go

I'll let the tears flow

Just flow… over my sadness

Until it is drowned from seeing tomorrow.

Irresistible

To receive my love, for you, is difficult

My love is steadfast, no matter what – that simple.

It remains constant and true in spite of all you do

To accept a love so incorruptible is improbable for you

It's difficult for you to grasp yet it has grips

There's nothing you've done to earn it

Therefore, there's nothing you can do to burn it

No distance between us deters it

Your resistance only delays its purpose

But my love stores up its energy for due time

Take this fruit, eat of it, and see that it is good

To deny my love given to you without limits,

Hurts my soul and insults my intellect.

I choose to see you wholesome and perfect

How do you view you?

I see that you are worthy of someone virtuous and noble.

What value do you place on yourself?

The issue is not that I love you too much

And you don't love me enough

There's no such thing allowed.

Love was never created in levels or amounts.

You can either let love live or die without it

You can not accept love, perfect harmony, God's love

Because you put stipulations and conditions on giving yours out; even to yourself.

My love is easy to bear.

The lightest weight you'll ever carry

The sweetest sound to make you merry

Full of hope, full of grace

With honest-to-God truth to emancipate

My love is easy to receive.

Just say "yes" and you will see

How deep.

How Deep

My love runs deep
So deep you could drown in it
So deep it would overtake you
So deep it reproduced another love
So that love could carry on the task of loving you more.
To the core of the earth,
Is how deep my love goes
Circling all the way around to itself
Doubling over itself
My love for you runs deep enough to withstand the tests
To conquer all doubts
To dispute any and all influences that steer you wrong
My love is always right
It hopes for the best
It is patient for you
It knows what will be, will be
And believes there is always a possibility of a positive outcome.
This love is so deep
It only wishes to be given away freely
With no returns or give-backs
What it gives is for you alone
There is no account kept
No thought of "I did this for you; you must do this for me."
My love is so deep
It loved you before the beginning of time
Before the thought ever entered into your mind
It was there
Waiting for the right time to pursue you
Getting the place prepared for where it would bring you
Studying your likes and dislikes, your favorites

To have everything organized to meet your most premium standard of comfort.

My love makes every effort to see you at your best potential

To speak only words that will inspire you

To encourage you to do better.

My love is so deep

It catches you when you fall

Cleans up the scrapes and wounds

Sends you back out to the battle

It strengthens your weaknesses

And moves beyond the "what happened"

And focuses almost completely on the "why it happened"

That's the deepness of my love

That's the fullness of its character

The realness of its kind

Nothing can compare to it in depth nor prestige.

My love is so deep

It has a firm foundation

No disaster or catastrophe could break it apart

You can anchor yourself to this love

Anchor your heart to the core of this love

You'll never feel unsure or insecure.

My love is so deep

Every time I offer it to you,

In every way that I show you,

You are coming into contact with the very essence of God

www.ingramcontent.com/pod-product-compliance
Lightning Source LLC
Chambersburg PA
CBHW032210040426
42449CB00005B/522